Real Estate Investing in 2023:

A Comprehensive Guide

Dawn-Marie Caputo

ISBN: 9798393472962

CONTENTS

Introduction

ACKNOWLEDGMENTS

I would like to express my deepest appreciation to everyone who has contributed to the making of this book on real estate investing in 2023. First and foremost, I would like to thank my family for their unwavering support and encouragement throughout the writing process. Without their love and support, this book would not have been possible.

I would like to express my gratitude to the team at Connected Investor for providing valuable insights and information on real estate investing, as well as access to their powerful PiN program. I would also like to thank my editor and proofreader for their meticulous work in ensuring that this book is clear, concise, and error-free. Finally, I would like to thank all the real estate investors and experts who have generously shared their knowledge and experience in this book. Your insights and expertise have been invaluable in helping readers understand the intricacies of real estate investing in 2023. It is my hope that this book will inspire and empower readers to achieve their real estate investing goals. Thank you all for your support and contributions.

INTRODUCTION

Real estate investing can be a lucrative way to build wealth over time. Whether you area seasoned investor or just getting started, there are a few key strategies you can use to make the most of your real estate investments. It involves purchasing, owning, managing, renting, and/or selling real estate properties for profit.

One of the main advantages of real estate investing is the potential for long-term appreciation. Unlike many other investments, real estate tends to increase in value over time, providing investors with a reliable source of capital appreciation. Additionally, real estate investing can provide a steady stream of passive income through rental income. By purchasing and renting out a property, investors can earn a regular income stream while also benefiting from long-term price appreciation.

However, investing in real estate also comes with its own set of risks and challenges. Real estate is a highly localized market, and fluctuations in the local economy, housing market, and regulatory environment can have a significant impact on property values and rental income. Additionally, real estate investing requires a significant upfront investment, and investors may need to take on significant debt to purchase properties. Finally, managing and maintaining real estate properties can be a time-consuming and complex process, requiring a high level of knowledge and expertise.

Despite these challenges, real estate investing can be a highly rewarding and lucrative investment strategy for those who are willing to put in the time and effort required. To get started in real estate investing, investors should start by researching different types of investments, including residential, commercial, and industrial properties, and determining which types of investments best align with their financial goals and risk tolerance.

Investors should also consider working with a real estate agent or broker who has experience in the local market and can provide guidance and support throughout the investment process.

Additionally, investors may want to consider partnering with other investors or investing in real estate investment trusts (REITs), which can provide diversification and reduce risk.

Real estate investing requires a significant amount of knowledge, expertise, and due diligence to be successful. However, for those who are willing to put in the work, real estate investing can provide a reliable source of long-term capital appreciation and passive income, making it an attractive investment option for a wide range of investors.

In this book, we will dive into the specifics of real estate investing in 2023, including market trends, financing options, and investment strategies.

1 - MARKET TRENDS

Real estate markets are constantly changing, and staying up to date on the latest trends is crucial for success in real estate investing. The year 2023 is expected to bring about several changes in the real estate market, driven by various economic, social, and environmental factors. In this article, we will explore some of the key real estate market trends that are likely to shape the industry in 2023. Increased demand for rental properties: With rising home prices, many people are opting to rent instead of buy. This has led to increased demand for rental properties, particularly in urban areas.

Continued Growth of the Housing Market

The housing market is expected to continue its growth trajectory in 2023, driven by a range of factors. The low interest rates and high demand for homes are expected to continue to fuel the housing market. Additionally, the millennial generation, which is now entering its prime home-buying years, is expected to continue to drive demand for housing. In fact, it is projected that by 2025, millennials will make up over 75% of the workforce, which will undoubtedly impact the housing market in the years to come.

Increased Focus on Sustainable & Eco-Friendly Building

Sustainability and eco-friendliness are becoming increasingly important in the real estate market. In 2023, we can expect to see an increased focus on green building practices, with more developers and builders incorporating environmentally friendly features into their projects. This will include everything from energy-efficient appliances and solar panels to green roofs and rainwater harvesting systems. The push towards sustainable building is being driven by both government regulations and consumer demand for eco-friendly homes.

The Rise of Co-Living Spaces

Co-living spaces have been gaining popularity in recent years, and this trend is expected to continue in 2023. Co-living spaces offer a unique living experience, with residents sharing communal spaces and amenities. This type of living arrangement is particularly attractive to young professionals, who are looking for affordable and flexible housing options. In addition, co-living spaces are often located in prime urban locations, making them a popular choice for those who want to be in the heart of the action.

Increased Use of Technology in Real Estate

Technology is playing an increasingly important role in the real estate industry, and this trend is also expected to continue in 2023. Real estate companies are using technology to streamline processes, improve customer experiences, and gain a competitive edge. This includes

everything from virtual property tours and online property listings to blockchain technology for property transactions. The use of technology is expected to increase efficiency in the industry and provide consumers with a more seamless experience.

Growth in the Luxury Real Estate Market

The luxury real estate market is expected to see continued growth in 2023. This is driven by a range of factors, including the growing wealth of high-net-worth individuals and the increasing demand for luxury properties in desirable locations. The luxury real estate market is expected to continue to see strong demand, particularly in urban areas and popular vacation destinations.

Increased Focus on Health and Wellness Amenities

Health and wellness amenities are becoming increasingly important in the real estate market. This year we can expect to see more developers incorporating fitness centers, yoga studios, and other health and wellness amenities into their projects. This is being driven by the growing interest in health and wellness among consumers, as well as the recognition that these amenities can add value to a property.

The Continued Rise of Smart Homes

Smart homes have been on the rise for several years, and this is expected to continue.Smart homes are designed to be more efficient, convenient, and secure, with features such as automated lighting, temperature control, and security systems. The increasing demand for smart homes is being driven by the growing interest in home automation and the desire for greater control over one's living environment.

The Emergence of New Real Estate Markets

New real estate markets are expected to emerge in 2023, as more investors and developers look for opportunities outside of traditional markets. This is being driven by several factors, including changing demographics, shifting economic conditions, and new technology. For example, the rise of remote work has led to a growing interest in real estate markets that offer a high quality of life and affordable living costs, even if they are not located in major urban centers.

Continued Growth of Commercial Real Estate

Commercial real estate is expected to continue its growth trajectory in 2023, as businesses continue to expand and look for new locations. The demand for office space, retail space, and industrial space is expected to remain strong, particularly in urban areas. Additionally, the rise of e-commerce has led to increased demand for warehouse and distribution space, as companies look for ways to store and ship their products efficiently.

Increased Investment in Real Estate Technology

Investment in real estate technology is expected to increase in 2023, as more companies look for ways to improve efficiency and gain a competitive edge. This includes investment in everything from artificial intelligence and machine learning to virtual and augmented reality. The use of technology is expected to transform the real estate industry in the years to come, with new tools and platforms being developed to streamline processes and improve customer experiences.

As you can see, the real estate market is expected to undergo significant changes in 2023, driven by a range of economic, social, and environmental factors. From the continued growth of the housing market to the emergence of new real estate markets and the increased use of technology, these trends are expected to shape the industry in the years to come. As the real estate market continues to evolve, it is important for investors, developers, and consumers to stay informed and adapt to these changes to succeed in the industry.

2 - FINANCING OPTIONS

One of the biggest challenges in real estate investing is financing your investments. There are several financing options available to real estate investors in 2023, including:

Traditional Mortgages

Traditional mortgages are still a popular option for real estate investors. With a traditional mortgage, you can finance up to 80% of the purchase price of a property. In 2023, these mortgages are expected to continue to play a significant role in the real estate market, as buyers and investors look to finance their purchases through traditional lending channels. Here are some of the key trends and developments in traditional real estate mortgages that are likely to impact the market in 2023.

Continued High Interest Rates

As of yesterday, these were the rates:

30-yr fixed - 7.254%

15-yr fixed - 6.214%

10/6 ARM - 7.203%

Mortgage rates can vary depending on a variety of factors, including economic conditions, lender policies, and borrower

characteristics. In general, there are several reasons why mortgage rates may be high at any given time. Here are some of the key factors that can contribute to high mortgage rates:

Economic Conditions

One of the primary factors that can impact mortgage rates is the overall state of the economy. When the economy is strong and growing, demand for borrowing tends to increase, which can lead to higher interest rates.

Conversely, when the economy is weak and struggling, interest rates may be lower to stimulate borrowing and economic growth.

Inflation

Inflation is another key factor that can impact mortgage rates. When inflation is high, lenders may raise interest rates to compensate for the decreased purchasing power of the currency. This can make borrowing more expensive, including mortgage lending.

Government Policies

Government policies can also have an impact on mortgage rates. For example, the Federal Reserve sets short-term interest rates, which can influence longer-term rates, such as those on mortgages. Additionally, government-backed mortgage programs, such as those offered by the Federal Housing Administration (FHA) or the Department of Veterans

Affairs (VA), may have different interest rate structures than traditional mortgage lenders.

Lender Policies

Lenders also play a significant role in determining mortgage rates. Some lenders may charge higher rates to manage risk, or to compensate for higher costs associated with lending.

Additionally, lenders may charge different rates based on the creditworthiness of the borrower, with lower rates typically reserved for borrowers with stronger credit histories and higher down payments.

Overall, mortgage rates can be influenced by a variety of factors, both economic and non-economic. While high mortgage rates can be a challenge for borrowers looking to finance a home purchase, it is important to understand the underlying factors that contribute to these rates to make informed borrowing decisions. Additionally, borrowers can work to improve their creditworthiness and financial situation to qualify for lower rates and more favorable mortgage terms.

Hard Money Loans & What They Are

Hard money loans are short-term loans that are typically used for fix-and-flip projects. These loans have higher interest rates and fees than traditional mortgages, but they can be easier to obtain. In 2023, hard money loans can offer investors a flexible financing option, but it is important to understand the terms and risks involved.

Hard money loans are a type of financing that is typically offered by private investors or companies, rather than traditional banks or lenders. These loans are usually short-term, ranging from a few months to a few years, and are secured by the property being purchased or renovated.

The terms of hard money loans are typically more flexible than traditional loans, but they also come with higher interest rates and fees. In addition, hard money lenders may require a larger down payment and may be more interested in the value of the property than the borrower's credit score or financial history.

Find a Hard Money Lender

If you are interested in getting a hard money loan, there are

several steps you can take:

Going to FastFundsNationwide.com is a wonderful way of getting a hard money loan. There are also many other private investors and companies that offer hard money loans.

Research potential lenders to find one that offers terms that fit your needs. Prepare your application: Hard money lenders typically require less documentation than traditional lenders, but you will need to provide information about the property you are purchasing, your experience as an investor, and your financial situation.

Present your proposal: Once you have found a potential lender and prepared your application, present your proposal for the property you are interested in purchasing or renovating. This may include an assessment of the property's value and a plan for renovation or resale.

Negotiate terms: If the lender is interested in working with you, you will need to negotiate the terms of the loan. This may include the interest rate, fees, and repayment schedule.

Close the loan: Once you have agreed to the terms, the lender will provide the funds for the loan. You will need to use the funds to purchase or renovate the property and make payments on the loan as agreed.

Benefits of Hard Money Loans

There are several benefits to using hard money loans,

including:

Quick Financing

Hard money loans can be approved and funded quickly, which can be important for real estate investors who need to act quickly on a property.

Flexibility

Hard money lenders are often more flexible than traditional lenders in terms of the type of property being purchased or renovated and the terms of the loan.

Access to Financing

Hard money loans can be an option for investors who may not qualify for traditional financing due to credit score or financial history.

Challenges of Hard Money Loans

While hard money loans can offer investors a flexible financing option, there are also some challenges to consider, including:

High interest rates and fees: Hard money loans typically come with higher interest rates and fees than traditional loans, which can increase the cost of the investment.

Short repayment period: Hard money loans are typically short-term, which means that investors will need to pay off the loan quickly or refinance it.

Risk of default: If an investor is unable to repay the loan, the hard money lender may foreclose on the property, which can result in the loss of the investment.

Hard money loans can be a flexible financing option for real estate investors who need quick funding or have difficulty qualifying for traditional financing. However, it is important to understand the terms and risks involved, including high interest rates and fees, short repayment periods, and the risk of default. Before applying for a hard money loan, it is important to thoroughly research potential lenders and have a solid plan for the property being purchased or renovated.

Crowdfunding

Crowdfunding is a new method of investing in real estate and has become an increasingly trendy way to finance real estate investments. With crowdfunding, investors pool their money together to fund a real estate project.

Real estate crowdfunding is a new method of investing in real estate that has become increasingly popular in recent years. It involves pooling funds from multiple investors to finance real estate projects, typically through an online platform. Here is an overview of what real estate crowdfunding is and how you can participate in it.

What is Real Estate Crowdfunding?

Real estate crowdfunding is a way for investors to participate in real estate projects without having to purchase an entire property themselves. Instead, investors can pool their money with other investors through an online platform and invest in a specific real estate project or portfolio. The platform acts as an intermediary, connecting investors with real estate developers and operators who are seeking financing for their projects.

There are two main types of real estate crowdfunding: debt and equity. Debt crowdfunding involves investors lending money to a real estate project and receiving interest payments in return. Equity crowdfunding involves investors buying a stake in a real estate project and sharing in the profits generated by the property. Both types of crowdfunding can offer investors an opportunity to diversify their portfolio and potentially earn higher returns than traditional investment options.

How to Participate in Real Estate Crowdfunding

Participating in real estate crowdfunding typically involves the following steps:

Choose a Platform: There are a growing number of real estate crowdfunding platforms available, each with their own investment options and fee structures. Before investing, it is important to research different platforms and choose one that aligns with your investment goals and risk tolerance.

Register and Verify Your Account: Once you have chosen a platform, you will typically need to register and verify your account. This may involve providing personal information, such as your name, address, and social security number, as well as providing proof of identity and income.

Browse Investment Opportunities: After your account has been verified, you can browse the investment opportunities available on the platform. This may include a range of real estate projects, such as commercial properties, residential developments, and multi-family housing.

Invest: Once you have identified an investment opportunity that meets your criteria, you can invest your funds through the platform. Depending on the platform, you may be able to invest as little as a few hundred dollars, or as much as several thousand.

Monitor Your Investment: After investing, it is important to monitor your investment and stay up to date on the progress of the real estate project. This may involve reviewing regular updates from the platform, as well as conducting your own research on the property and its performance.

Benefits and Risks of Real Estate Crowdfunding

Real estate crowdfunding offers a range of potential benefits for investors, including the ability to diversify their portfolio, potentially earn higher returns than traditional investment options, and participate in real estate projects that would otherwise be inaccessible. However, there are also risks involved, including the potential for loss of investment, lack of liquidity, and the need to conduct thorough due diligence before investing.

Real estate crowdfunding can be a viable option for investors who are looking to diversify their portfolio and potentially earn higher returns than traditional investment options.

However, it is important to conduct thorough research and due diligence before investing, and to carefully consider the risks and potential rewards associated with each investment opportunity.

3 - INVESTMENT STRATEGIES

There are several different investment strategies you can use in real estate investing, depending on your goals and risk tolerance. Here are a few common strategies in 2023:

Buy and Hold

The buy and hold strategy is a classic approach to real estate investing that involves purchasing a property and holding onto it for the long term. The goal of this strategy is to generate passive income through rental income and appreciation of the property over time.

To make the buy and hold strategy work, it is important to carefully research and choose a property that is likely to increase in value over time and generate strong rental income. This may involve selecting a property in a growing market with high demand for rental properties, or a property that can be improved or renovated to increase its value.

BRRRR

The BRRRR method is a popular real estate investment strategy that stands for *Buy, Rehab, Rent, Refinance, and Repeat*. This strategy is designed to help investors acquire and hold rental properties while maximizing their returns.

Here I show the BRRRR method works:

Buy: The first step is to identify and purchase a property that has the potential to generate positive cash flow. The property may need some rehab work, but it should be priced low enough to provide a good return on investment.

Rehab: Once you have acquired the property, it is time to rehab it to increase its value and attract higher-paying tenants. This may involve making repairs, updating the interior or exterior, or adding new amenities that will appeal to renters.

Rent: With the property rehabbed and ready to go, the next step is to find and secure a tenant. This may involve advertising the property on rental listing websites, working with a property management company, or networking with local real estate professionals.

Refinance: Once the property is rented, it is time to refinance the mortgage to take advantage of the increased value. By refinancing, you can pull out some of the equity from the property and use it to reinvest in other properties.

Repeat: With the mortgage refinanced, you can use the proceeds to acquire and rehab another property, repeating the process repeatedly.

The BRRRR method has several benefits for real estate investors. First, it allows investors to acquire properties with little or no money down, which can help them build a portfolio quickly. Second, it allows investors to increase the value of their properties through rehab work, which can lead to higher rental income and increased equity. Finally, it allows investors to refinance their properties and use the proceeds to invest in additional properties, creating a virtuous cycle of growth and expansion.

To successfully implement the BRRRR method, it is important to be strategic and patient. Finding the right property at the right price can take time, as can rehabbing and renting the property. It is important to have a clear investment strategy in place and to be disciplined in following it. This may involve working with a team of real estate professionals, including a real estate agent, contractor, property manager, and mortgage broker.

Flipping

The flipping method of real estate investing involves purchasing a property, making repairs or renovations, and then selling it quickly for a profit. This strategy is popular among investors who are looking for a short-term investment opportunity that can generate high returns.

Purchase a property: The first step is to identify and purchase a property that has the potential to generate a good return on investment. This may involve working with a real estate agent or scouring online listings for distressed or undervalued properties.

Make repairs or renovations: Once you've acquired the property, the next step is to make any necessary repairs or renovations to increase its value. This may involve updating the kitchen or bathrooms, adding new flooring or paint, or making structural repairs.

Sell the Property

With the repairs or renovations complete, the next step is to sell the property quickly for a profit. This may involve listing the property for sale with a real estate agent, advertising it on online listing platforms, or networking with other real estate professionals to find potential buyers.

The flipping method can be a lucrative investment strategy if executed properly, but it also comes with some risks. One of the main challenges of flipping is accurately estimating the cost of repairs and renovations. If you underestimate these costs, your profit margins could be significantly reduced. Additionally, the real estate market can be unpredictable, and there is always a risk that you may not be able to sell the property quickly or for the price you were hoping for.

To successfully execute the flipping method, it's important to have a solid investment plan in place and to work with a team of professionals who can help you navigate the process. This may include a real estate agent, contractor, property inspector, and accountant. It's also important to be patient and disciplined in your approach, and to avoid taking on too much risk or making impulsive decisions.

Another key factor in successful flipping is market knowledge. It is important to stay up to date on real estate trends and market conditions in your area, as well as to have a strong understanding of the local housing market. This can help you make informed decisions about which properties to invest in and how to price them for sale.

Real Estate Investment Trusts (REITs)

Real Estate Investment Trusts (REITs) are a popular investment vehicle in the real estate industry. A REIT is a company that owns, operates, or finances income-producing real estate properties. Investing in REITs allows individuals to own a portion of a diversified portfolio of real estate assets without having to purchase and manage properties themselves.

Types of REITs

There are several types of REITs, including equity REITs, mortgage REITs, and hybrid REITs. Equity REITs own and operate income-producing properties, while mortgage REITs invest in mortgages and mortgage-backed securities. Hybrid REITs invest in both properties and mortgages.

Equity REITs

Equity REITs are the most common type of REIT. They own and operate income-generating real estate properties, such as apartment buildings, office buildings, shopping centers, and hotels. Equity REITs generate income from rental payments and capital gains from selling properties. They typically pay out at least 90% of their taxable income as dividends to their shareholders, which makes them an attractive option for income-seeking investors.

Mortgage REITs

Mortgage REITs, also known as mREITs, invest in mortgages and mortgage-backed securities. They do not own real estate properties but instead lend money to property owners or invest in mortgages. Their income comes from the interest earned on the mortgages they hold,or the fees charged for originating or servicing mortgages. Mortgage REITs typically have higher yields than equity REITs, but they also carry higher risks due to their exposure to interest rate fluctuations and credit risk.

Hybrid REITs

Hybrid REITs invest in both real estate properties and mortgages. They provide investors with a diversified exposure to the real estate market, with the potential for both rental income and interest income. Hybrid REITs can be further divided into two subcategories: equity-oriented hybrid REITs and mortgage-oriented hybrid REITs.

Equity-oriented hybrid REITs have a higher proportion of real estate assets, while mortgage-oriented hybrid REITs have a higher proportion of mortgage assets.

Public Non-Listed REITs

Public Non-Listed REITs (PNLRs) are registered with the Securities and Exchange Commission (SEC) but are not listed on public stock exchanges. They are sold through brokers and financial advisors and are only available to accredited investors. PNLRs typically have lower fees and higher yields than publicly traded REITs but are less liquid and have less transparency.

Private REITs

Private REITs are not registered with the SEC and are only available to a limited number of investors. They are typically sold through private placements to accredited investors, institutional investors, or high net worth individuals. Private REITs have the potential for higher returns than publicly traded REITs, but they also carry higher risks due to their lack of regulation and transparency.

Exchange-Traded REITs

Exchange-Traded REITs (ETFs) are publicly traded on stock exchanges, and investors can buy and sell shares like they would with any other stock. ETFs provide investors with the benefits of real estate investing, such as diversification and potential income, without the liquidity constraints of traditional real estate investments. ETFs are easy to trade and have lower fees than other types of REITs, but they can be volatile and may not provide the same level of diversification as other types of REITs.

International REITs

International REITs invest in real estate assets located outside of the United States. They provide investors with exposure to global real estate markets and can offer higher returns than domestic REITs. However, investing in international REITs carries additional risks, such as currency fluctuations, political instability, and different regulatory environments.

Here are Some Key Points to Understand about REITs

Income Potential: One of the main benefits of investing in REITs is the potential for income generation. REITs are required to distribute at least 90% of their taxable income to shareholders as dividends, making them an attractive option for income-seeking investors.

Diversification

Another benefit of REITs is the ability to diversify your real estate portfolio. By investing in a REIT, you can own a portion of a diversified portfolio of properties across different asset classes, geographies, and sectors.

Liquidity

REITs are traded on major stock exchanges, making them a liquid investment. Investors can buy and sell shares of REITs at any time, allowing them to easily adjust their real estate portfolio based on market conditions.

Risk Factors

Like any investment, REITs come with certain risks. One risk is the potential for interest rate fluctuations, which can impact on the cost of borrowing for REITs and the value of their assets. Another risk is the potential for economic downturns, which can impact the demand for real estate properties and the ability of REITs to generate income.

When investing in REITs, it is important to do your due diligence and research the specific company and its portfolio of properties. Look at factors such as the type of properties the REIT invests in, its financial performance, and the record of accomplishment of its management team.

Additionally, it is important to consider the fees associated with investing in a REIT. Some REITs charge high fees, which can eat into your potential returns. Be sure to read the prospectus and understand the fees associated with the investment before deciding.

Vacation Rentals & Airbnb

Vacation rentals can be a lucrative real estate investment strategy for investors in areas with high demand for short-term rentals. This may involve purchasing a property in a popular vacation destination, such as a beach town or ski resort, and renting it out to vacationers through platforms like Airbnb.

To make vacation rentals work, it is important to carefully research the local market and identify a property that can generate strong rental income during peak seasons. It is also important to consider the costs associated with managing and maintaining the property, including cleaning, repairs, and marketing.

Investing in a property for use as an Airbnb rental can be a lucrative real estate investment strategy, particularly in areas with high demand for short-term rentals. To make this strategy work, it is important to carefully research the local market and identify a property that can generate strong rental income during peak seasons. It is also important to consider the costs associated with managing and maintaining the property, including cleaning, repairs, and marketing. A successful Airbnb investment strategy may involve working with a property management company to ensure the property is effectively managed and marketed to maximize rental income.

Commercial Real Estate

Commercial real estate investments involve purchasing properties such as office buildings, retail spaces, and warehouses for the purpose of generating passive income through leasing and capital appreciation. Commercial real estate investments can offer higher returns than residential real estate, but also come with higher risk due to the typically larger scale and more complex management requirements. To make commercial real estate investments work, it is important to carefully research the local market and identify properties that are likely to generate strong rental income and increase in value over time. It is also important to consider the costs associated with managing and maintaining the property, including tenant management, repairs, and marketing.

Commercial real estate investments can offer a range of benefits, including potential for higher returns, diversification of a portfolio, and the ability to leverage debt to increase returns. One common approach to commercial real estate investment is to purchase a property and lease it out to tenants. This requires careful management of tenants and rental income, as well as maintenance and repairs of the property.

Another option for commercial real estate investment is to participate in a Real Estate Investment Trust (REIT). REITs are publicly traded companies that invest in a portfolio of commercial real estate assets, and investors can buy shares of the REIT to receive a portion of the income generated by the properties in the portfolio.

Overall, commercial real estate investments can be a valuable addition to an investment portfolio, but it is important to carefully research and understand the market and associated risks before investing. Working with a professional real estate advisor or broker can help ensure a successful investment strategy.

Real estate investing can be a wonderful way to build wealth over time. By staying up to date on the latest market trends, financing options, and investment strategies, you can make the most of your real estate investments in 2023 and beyond. Whether you are a seasoned investor or just getting started, there has never been a better time to invest in real estate.

4 - FINDING & ANALYZING PROPERTIES

Finding and analyzing properties is a critical step in real estate investing. In 2023, there are several ways to find properties, including:

Online Listing Platforms

The advent of online real estate platforms has made it easier than ever for investors to find and analyze potential investment properties. These platforms offer a wealth of information on properties for sale, including photos, descriptions, and financial data. Here are some tips for finding and analyzing properties on online listing platforms:

Use Filters

Most online listing platforms allow users to filter properties by a range of criteria, such as price range, location, property type, and more. This can help you quickly narrow down your search and focus on properties that meet your specific investment goals.

Check the Property History

Most online listing platforms will provide a history of the property, including previous sales, tax assessments, and other important data. This can help you get a better understanding of the property's value and potential for appreciation.

Review Property Details

Pay close attention to the property details provided on the listing, including square footage, number of bedrooms and bathrooms, and any other key features. This will help you determine whether the property is a good fit for your investment strategy.

Analyze Financial Data

Many online listing platforms will provide financial data on the property, such as rental income, expenses, and potential cash flow. Be sure to carefully review this information and factor it into your investment analysis.

Conduct due diligence: Once you have identified a property that you are interested in, it is important to conduct a thorough due diligence process to ensure that it is a sound investment. This may involve hiring a professional inspector, reviewing local zoning and land use regulations, and researching the local market and comparable properties.

Overall, online listing platforms can be a valuable tool for finding and analyzing potential investment properties. However, it is important to exercise caution and carefully review all available information before making an investment decision. Working with a professional real estate advisor or broker can help ensure a successful investment strategy.

Websites like Zillow and Redfin allow you to search for properties by location, price, and other criteria.

Real Estate Agents

Real estate agents can be a valuable resource for investors looking to find and analyze potential investment properties. Here are some tips for finding and analyzing properties via real estate agents:

Choose the Right Agent

Look for a real estate agent who specializes in investment properties and has experience working with investors. This can help ensure that they understand your investment goals and can provide valuable guidance throughout the process.

Communicate your Investment Criteria

Be clear with your real estate agent about the types of properties you are interested in, such as location, property type, and price range. This will help them narrow down their search and identify properties that meet your criteria.

Review property details: Once your agent has identified potential investment properties, review the property details provided on the listing. Pay close attention to features such as square footage, number of bedrooms and bathrooms, and any other vital details. This will help you determine whether the property is a good fit for your investment strategy.

Analyze Financial Data

Your real estate agent may be able to provide financial data on the property, such as rental income, expenses, and potential cash flow. Be sure to carefully review this information and factor it into your investment analysis.

Conduct Due Diligence

Once you have identified a property that you are interested in, it is important to conduct a thorough due diligence process to ensure that it is a sound investment. This may involve hiring a professional inspector, reviewing local zoning and land use regulations, and researching the local market and comparable properties.

Negotiate the Deal

Your real estate agent can help you negotiate the deal with the seller or their agent. Be sure to have a clear understanding of the terms of the agreement, including any contingencies or warranties.

Close the Deal

Once the deal has been negotiated, work with your real estate agent to complete the closing process. This may involve hiring an attorney, obtaining financing, and completing any necessary paperwork.

Overall, working with a real estate agent can be a valuable resource for finding and analyzing potential investment properties. Be sure to choose an agent who understands your investment goals and has experience of working with investors. Communicate your investment criteria clearly and conduct thorough due diligence to ensure a successful investment strategy.

Direct Mail Marketing

Sending direct mail to homeowners in a specific area can be an effective way to find off-market properties. This can be an effective way for investors to find potential investment properties. Here are some tips for finding and analyzing properties via direct mail marketing:

Define your Target Market

Before launching a direct mail marketing campaign, it is important to define your target market. This may involve identifying specific neighborhoods or property types that align with your investment strategy.

Build a Targeted List

Once you have defined your target market, build a list of potential properties to target. This may involve using public records, such as tax assessments or deed records, to identify properties that meet your criteria.

Create a compelling message: Your direct mail marketing message should be compelling and targeted to your audience. Consider using language that speaks to the specific needs or pain points of property owners in your target market.

Send your Mailer

Once your message is crafted and your list is built, send your mailer to potential property owners. Be sure to track your response rates and adjust your message or target market as needed.

Analyze Responses

When you receive responses to your direct mail campaign, it is important to analyze the properties to determine whether they meet your investment criteria. This may involve conducting due diligence on the property, including reviewing public records, inspecting the property, and researching the local market.

Negotiate the Deal

Once you have identified a property that meets your investment criteria, work with the seller to negotiate the deal. Be sure to have a clear understanding of the terms of the agreement, including any contingencies or warranties.

Close the Deal

Once the deal has been negotiated, work with the seller to complete the closing process. This may involve hiring an attorney, obtaining financing, and completing any necessary paperwork.

Overall, direct mail marketing can be an effective way for investors to find potential investment properties. By defining your target market, building a targeted list, creating a compelling message, and analyzing responses, you can identify properties that align with your investment strategy.

Be sure to conduct thorough due diligence and negotiate the deal carefully to ensure a successful investment.

Once you have found a property, it is important to analyze it thoroughly before making an offer. This includes looking at factors like:

The property's location: The location of a property can have a significant impact on its value and potential for appreciation.

The property's condition: The condition of a property can affect how much work and money you will need to invest to get it ready for rental or resale.

The property's income potential: If you are investing in rental properties, it is important to look at the potential rental income to ensure it will be a profitable investment.

Purchasing Notes on Homes

Purchasing notes on homes is an alternative form of real estate investing that allows investors to earn a return without owning the property. Essentially, an investor purchases the debt owed on a property rather than the property itself.

What are Notes?

A note is a legal document that represents a debt owed on a property. It is an IOU that the borrower signs to promise to pay back the loan. The note includes the loan amount, interest rate, payment schedule, and other terms of the loan.

How to Purchase Notes on Homes?

Investors can purchase notes on homes from banks, mortgage lenders, or other note holders. Notes can be purchased at a discount, meaning the investor pays less than the face value of the note. The discount reflects the risk and uncertainty associated with collecting the debt owed.

Why Invest in Notes on Homes?

Investing in notes on homes can be an attractive option for investors who are looking for a passive income stream without the responsibilities of owning and managing a property. If the borrower continues to make their payments, the investor earns a regular stream of income from the interest paid on the note. Additionally, if the borrower defaults on the loan, the investor can foreclose on the property and take ownership of the home.

Risks of Purchasing Notes on Homes

As with any investment, there are risks associated with purchasing notes on homes. The primary risk is that the borrower will default on the loan, leaving the investor with a non-performing asset. Additionally, there may be legal and regulatory risks associated with foreclosing on a property. Investors must carefully assess the creditworthiness of the borrower and the value of the property before investing in a note.

How to Find Notes to Purchase

If you are interested in purchasing notes on homes, the first step is to find notes that are available for purchase. Here are some ways to find notes to purchase:

Banks and Lenders

One of the most common sources of notes on homes is banks and mortgage lenders. These institutions may have non-performing loans or distressed assets on their books that they are looking to sell. You can reach out to these institutions directly or work with a broker who has connections in the industry.

Online Marketplaces

There are also online marketplaces where you can find notes on homes for sale. Websites such as NoteMarketplace.com and Paperstac.com allow investors to browse and purchase notes on homes from around the country. These marketplaces provide transparency and convenience, making it easier for investors to find and purchase notes.

Networking

Networking can also be an effective way to find notes to purchase. Attend real estate investment clubs, conferences, and other industry events to connect with other investors, brokers, and lenders. Let people know that you are interested in purchasing notes on homes and see if they have any leads or referrals.

Direct Mail

Another strategy is to send direct mail to homeowners who are in default on their mortgages. You can use public records to find these homeowners and send them a letter expressing your interest in purchasing their note. While this strategy may require some time and effort, it can be an effective way to find off-market opportunities. Finding notes to purchase requires some effort and diligence, but there are many sources available to investors.

Banks and lenders, online marketplaces, networking, and direct mail are all strategies that investors can use to find notes on homes for sale. Regardless of the strategy you choose, it is important to conduct thorough due diligence and work with professionals who can help you assess the risks and potential returns of each investment opportunity.

Risks of Purchasing Notes on Homes

As with any investment, purchasing notes on a home can be a tempting investment opportunity for real estate investors. However, there are several risks that investors should be aware of before they decide to buy these types of investments.

One risk is the possibility of default. If the borrower on the note is unable to make payments, the investor will not receive the expected returns. Furthermore, the process of foreclosing on a property can be lengthy and expensive, leaving the investor with an illiquid asset that may not generate a return for several months or even years.

Another risk is the potential for fraud. Not all notes on homes are legitimate, and some may be frauds designed to swindle investors out of their money. Investors should thoroughly research the note and the borrower before making any investment decisions.

Additionally, purchasing notes on homes can be a complex and opaque process. Investors may not have access to all the information they need to make an informed decision, such as the borrower's credit history and financial situation.

Finally, the value of a note can be affected by changes in the real estate market. If property values decline, the value of the note may also decrease, potentially leaving the investor with a loss.

Despite these risks, there are still opportunities for investors to profit from purchasing notes on homes. By conducting thorough due diligence and carefully assessing the risks, investors can potentially earn high returns on their investment. However, investors should approach these investments with caution and only invest money they can afford to lose.

5 - MANAGING YOUR INVESTMENTS

Once you have purchased a property, managing it effectively is key to long-term success. In 2023, there are several tools and resources available to help you manage your real estate investments, including:

Property management software: There are several software options available that can help you manage your rental properties more efficiently, from tracking rent payments to scheduling maintenance tasks.

Real estate investment groups: Joining a real estate investment group can give you access to resources and support from other investors.

Outsourcing

Outsourcing tasks like property management or maintenance can help you save time and focus on the big picture of your real estate investments.

Real estate investing in 2023 offers a variety of opportunities for investors, from rental properties to fix-and-flip projects to REITs. By staying up to date on market trends, financing options, and investment strategies, you can make the most of your investments and build long-term wealth. Remember to thoroughly analyze properties before making an offer and to manage your investments effectively to ensure continued success. The best out there is ConnectedInvestor.com.

An Overview of the Real Estate Investing Platform

ConnectedInvestor.com is a real estate investing platform that connects investors, lenders, wholesalers, and other real estate professionals. The platform provides access to a wide range of real estate investment opportunities, education, and networking opportunities.

Features of Connected Investor

Real Estate Investment Opportunities: Connected Investor provides access to a wide range of real estate investment opportunities, including off-market properties, wholesale deals, fix-and-flip properties, rental properties, and commercial properties. Investors can use the platform to browse and search for properties based on location, property type, and investment criteria.

Funding Options: Connected Investor also provides access to a variety of funding options, including hard money loans, private money loans, and crowdfunding. Investors can apply for funding directly through the platform or connect with lenders and investors who are interested in funding their deals.

Education and Training: Connected Investor provides a variety of educational resources and training programs to help investors learn about real estate investing and improve their skills. These resources include webinars, podcasts, articles, and courses on topics such as wholesaling, rehabbing, financing, and marketing.

<u>Networking and Community</u>: Connected Investor provides a platform for real estate professionals to connect and network with each other. Investors can join local real estate investment clubs, attend networking events, and connect with other members through the platform's messaging system.

<u>Software Tools</u>: Connected Investor also provides a variety of software tools to help investors manage their real estate investing business. These tools include a deal analyzer, a property listing platform, and a CRM system to manage contacts and leads.

<u>The PiN Program on Connected Investor- An Overview</u>: The PiN Program (Property Investment Navigators) is a proprietary software tool offered by Connected Investor to help real estate investors find off-market properties, leads, and investment opportunities. The PiN program uses a combination of data analytics and machine learning algorithms to scan and analyze millions of property records across the United States, providing investors with a comprehensive list of properties that fit their investment criteria.

Features of the PiN Program

<u>Off-Market Properties</u>: The PiN program provides access to a wide range of off-market properties, including pre-foreclosures, foreclosures, bank-owned properties, and properties with motivated sellers. These properties are not listed on the MLS or other public real estate listing platforms, making them a valuable source of investment opportunities.

Advanced Search Filters: The PiN program allows investors to filter their property search based on a variety of criteria, including location, property type, price range, and investment strategy. Investors can customize their search to target specific neighborhoods, property types, and investment criteria.

Property Data Analytics: The PiN program provides investors with detailed property data analytics, including estimated property values, rental rates, and rehab costs. This data helps investors make informed decisions about which properties to invest in and how much to offer.

Automated Lead Generation: The PiN program uses machine learning algorithms to automate lead generation, allowing investors to receive notifications and alerts for new properties that match their investment criteria. This saves investors time and effort in manually searching for properties and leads.

Training and Support: Connected Investor offers training and support to help investors learn how to use the PiN program effectively and make the most of its features. The platform provides educational resources, webinars, and customer support to assist investors with their real estate investing goals.

Go here for a free trial. You will love it!

6 - TAX CONSIDERATIONS

When it comes to investing in real estate, it is important to be aware of the tax implications. Here are some of the key tax considerations to keep in mind when investing in real estate:

Depreciation

One of the most significant tax benefits of investing in real estate is depreciation. Depreciation allows you to deduct a portion of the property's cost each year over its useful life as a way of accounting for the property's wear and tear. This deduction can reduce your taxable income and lower your tax bill.

Capital Gains Taxes

If you sell a property for a profit, you will be subject to capital gains taxes. However, if you hold the property for more than a year before selling, you may be eligible for long-term capital gains tax rates, which are typically lower than short-term capital gains rates.

1031 Exchanges

A 1031 exchange is a tax-deferred exchange that allows you to sell a property and reinvest the proceeds into a new property, deferring the capital gains tax until you sell the new property. To qualify for a 1031 exchange, the new property must be of equal or greater value, and the exchange must be completed within a certain time.

Passive Activity Rules

If you own a rental property, you may be subject to passive activity rules, which limit the number of losses you can deduct from your taxable income. These rules are designed to prevent taxpayers from using real estate losses to offset other types of income.

Rental Income Taxes

If you own a rental property, you will be required to pay taxes on the rental income you receive. This income is subject to ordinary income tax rates, and you may also be subject to self-employment taxes if you actively manage the property.

Real estate professional status: If you are actively involved in the management of your real estate properties and meet certain criteria, you may be eligible for real estate professional status. This status allows you to deduct real estate losses against your other types of income without being subject to the passive activity rules.

State and local taxes: In addition to federal taxes, you will also be subject to state and local taxes on your real estate investments. These taxes can vary widely depending on the state and locality in which you invest, so it is important to research the tax rates and regulations in your area.

It is important to consult with a tax professional when investing in real estate to ensure that you are complying with all relevant tax laws and regulations. A tax professional can also help you identify potential tax savings and strategies to maximize your returns.

Additionally, it is important to keep accurate records of all your real estate transactions and expenses to make tax time easier and to help you take advantage of all available tax deductions and credits.

Opportunity Zones

Opportunity Zones are designated geographic areas in the United States that offer tax incentives to investors who invest in businesses and real estate within those areas. The Opportunity Zone program was created as part of the 2017 Tax Cuts and Jobs Act to encourage economic development in distressed communities.

One of the key benefits of investing in Opportunity Zones is the potential for tax savings. Investors can defer capital gains taxes on investments in Opportunity Zones until the end of 2026, or until they sell their investment, whichever comes first. Additionally, if the investment is held for at least 10 years, any appreciation in value is tax-free.

The tax incentives offered by Opportunity Zones can make real estate investing in these areas an attractive option for investors. However, it is important to thoroughly research and analyze any potential investment to ensure that it aligns with your investment goals and risk tolerance.

It is also important to note that while Opportunity Zones offer tax incentives, they are not a guaranteed investment opportunity. Investors should carefully evaluate the potential risks and rewards of any investment and seek the advice of financial and tax professionals before making any investment decisions.

7 - RISKS & CHALLENGES

Real estate investing comes with its fair share of risks and challenges. Real estate investing can be a lucrative way to build wealth and generate passive income, but it is important to be aware of the risks and challenges that come with this type of investment. In 2023, some of the common risks and challenges include:

Market Risk

Real estate markets can be volatile and subject to economic and political factors that can impact property values. A downturn in the market can result in a decrease in property values, rental income, and cash flow.

Financing Risk

Real estate investments often require significant capital, and obtaining financing can be challenging. Interest rates can also impact the profitability of a real estate investment, particularly if rates rise significantly.

Management Risk

Real estate investments require ongoing management, maintenance, and upkeep, which can be time-consuming and costly. Poor management can lead to higher vacancy rates, lower rental income, and higher expenses.

Tenant Risk

Tenants can pose a significant risk to real estate investments. Non-payment of rent, damage to the property, and early lease termination can all impact cash flow and profitability.

Regulatory Risk

Real estate investments are subject to local and state regulations, including zoning laws, building codes, and rental laws. Changes in regulations can impact the profitability of a real estate investment.

Environmental Risk

Environmental issues such as contamination, flooding, and other natural disasters can impact the value of a real estate investment.

Legal Risk

Real estate investments can be subject to legal disputes, including contract disputes, tenant lawsuits, and property damage claims. Legal fees and settlements can be costly and impact profitability.

Liquidity Risk

Real estate investments are less liquid than other types of investments. It can be challenging to sell a property quickly if cash is needed, and a long sales process can impact cash flow.

Overleveraging Risk

Taking on too much debt to finance a real estate investment can result in financial difficulties if cash flow decreases or interest rates rise.

Market Timing Risk

Timing the real estate market can be challenging, and investing at the wrong time can result in lower returns or losses. To mitigate these risks and challenges, it is important to conduct thorough research and analysis before making any real estate investment. This includes researching the local market, understanding financing options, carefully managing the property, and working with experienced professionals, such as real estate agents, property managers, and attorneys.

It is also important to have a solid financial plan and to be prepared for unexpected expenses or fluctuations in cash flow. Diversifying investments across multiple properties and markets can also help to mitigate risk.

Real estate investing in 2023 can be a profitable way to build wealth, but it is important to be aware of the risks and challenges involved and to take steps to mitigate those risks.

With careful planning and management, real estate investments can provide a steady stream of passive income and long-term appreciation.

8 - Real Estate Investing for Different

Goals: Real estate investing can be pursued for different goals, and it is important to understand how to tailor your strategy to meet those goals. Real estate investing can be a fantastic way to build wealth, generate passive income, and achieve financial goals.In 2023, some of the most common goals for real estate investing include:

Building Wealth

One common goal of real estate investing is to build long-term wealth. This can be achieved by purchasing properties that are expected to appreciate over time, generating passive rental income, and potentially selling the properties for a profit in the future. This strategy often involves a long-term investment horizon and a focus on cash flow rather than immediate returns.

Generating passive income: Real estate investing can also be a terrific way to generate passive income. This can be achieved by purchasing rental properties that generate regular rental income. Investors can also consider strategies such as short-term rentals, like Airbnb, or commercial properties, like retail or office space, that generate regular lease payments.

Diversifying Investments

Real estate can be a valuable addition to a diversified investment portfolio. Investors can consider investing in real estate investment trusts (REITs), which allow investors to invest in real estate without owning physical property.

Investors can also consider purchasing properties in different markets or investing in diverse types of properties, like commercial, residential, or industrial.

Achieving financial independence: Many real estate investors seek to achieve financial independence by generating enough passive income from real estate investments to cover their expenses. This can be achieved through a combination of rental income, appreciation, and potentially selling properties for a profit. Investors may need to purchase multiple properties or invest in higher-income properties to achieve this goal.

Retirement Planning

Real estate investing can also be a terrific way to plan for retirement. By purchasing properties that generate regular rental income, investors can create a source of retirement income. Real estate can also be a valuable addition to a retirement portfolio, providing diversification and potential appreciation over time.

When pursuing these different goals, it is important to have a clear investment strategy and to conduct thorough research and analysis before making any investments. This includes researching local markets, understanding financing options, carefully managing properties, and working with experienced professionals like real estate agents, property managers, and attorneys.

Investors should also have a clear understanding of their financial goals and risk tolerance. Some investment strategies, like flipping properties for a quick profit, may be higher risk but offer higher potential returns, while other strategies, like purchasing rental properties, may offer lower risk but more modest returns.

Real estate investing can be a valuable addition to a well-diversified investment portfolio, but it is important to carefully consider investment goals and strategies and to approach investments with a long-term perspective. By doing so, investors can potentially achieve their financial goals and build long-term wealth through real estate investing.

Passive Income

Investing in rental properties can provide a steady stream of passive income, which can be a fantastic way to supplement your income or build wealth over time. Real estate investing with passive goals typically involves purchasing properties that generate regular rental income, allowing investors to earn passive income without actively managing the properties. This can be a wonderful way to generate income without the time commitment of actively managing a property or the risk of actively flipping properties.

Investors pursuing passive real estate investing goals may choose to purchase rental properties that are already generating income, rather than purchasing properties that require significant renovations or improvements. They may also choose to invest in commercial properties that generate regular lease payments or consider real estate investment trusts (REITs), which allow investors to invest in real estate without owning physical property.

When pursuing passive real estate investing goals, it is important to carefully research and analyze potential investments to ensure they are likely to generate regular income and offer potential for long-term appreciation. Investors should also carefully manage their properties, including screening tenants, ensuring properties are properly maintained, and addressing any tenant concerns or issues in a timely manner.

Overall, passive real estate investing can be a fantastic way to generate income and build long-term wealth, but it is important to approach investments with a clear strategy and a long-term perspective. By doing so, investors can potentially achieve their financial goals and earn passive income through real estate investing.

Capital Appreciation

Investing in properties with strong potential for appreciation can help you build wealth through appreciation of the property value. Real estate investing with capital appreciation goals involves purchasing properties with the intention of selling them for a profit in the future. This strategy typically involves investing in properties that are undervalued or have significant potential for appreciation, such as properties located in up-and-coming neighborhoods or those that require significant renovations.

Investors pursuing capital appreciation goals may choose to purchase properties that are below market value, with the intention of improving the properties and selling them for a profit. Alternatively, they may choose to invest in properties that are expected to appreciate over time, such as those located in areas with strong economic growth or those with desirable amenities.

When pursuing capital appreciation goals, it is important to carefully research and analyze potential investments to ensure they have strong potential for appreciation and offer a good return on investment. Investors should also be prepared to actively manage their properties, including overseeing renovations or improvements, and marketing the properties for sale.

Overall, real estate investing with capital appreciation goals can be a wonderful way to potentially achieve significant returns on investment over time. However, it is important to approach investments with a clear strategy, a long-term perspective, and a willingness to actively manage properties to maximize their potential for appreciation.

Diversification

Real estate investing with diversification goals involves purchasing a mix of diverse types of properties to spread risk and create a well-rounded portfolio. This strategy typically involves investing in a mix of different property types, such as residential, commercial, and industrial properties, as well as properties located in different regions or markets.

Investors pursuing diversification goals may choose to purchase properties in different markets or regions to reduce their exposure to any one market or region. Additionally, they may choose to invest in different property types to reduce their exposure to any one particular property type.

When pursuing diversification goals, it is important to carefully research and analyze potential investments to ensure they offer a good return on investment and align with the investor's overall portfolio strategy. Additionally, investors should be prepared to actively manage their properties, including overseeing tenant relationships, property maintenance, and rental income.

Overall, real estate investing with diversification goals can be a great way to reduce risk and build a well-rounded portfolio. However, it is important to approach investments with a clear strategy, a long-term perspective, and a willingness to actively manage properties to maximize their potential for success.

Retirement Planning

Real estate investing with retirement planning goals involves purchasing properties with the intention of generating a steady stream of passive income in retirement. This strategy typically involves investing in rental properties that can generate consistent rental income over a prolonged period of time. It can help you build a nest egg for retirement.

Investors pursuing retirement planning goals may choose to invest in properties that are in areas with strong rental demand, have stable tenant populations, and offer good potential for long-term appreciation. They may also focus on properties that can be paid off over time, generating a steady stream of rental income in retirement.

When pursuing retirement planning goals, it is important to carefully research and analyze potential investments to ensure they offer a good return on investment and align with the investor's overall retirement strategy. Additionally, investors should be prepared to actively manage their properties or work with a property management company to ensure consistent rental income.

Overall, real estate investing with retirement planning goals can be a great way to generate passive income in retirement and potentially achieve long-term financial security.

However, it is important to approach investments with a clear strategy, a long-term perspective, and a willingness to actively manage properties to maximize their potential for success.

9 - WHOLESALING PROPERTIES

Wholesaling properties is a popular real estate investing strategy in which investors find distressed properties, put them under contract, and then assign the contract to another investor for a fee. In 2023, wholesaling properties can be a profitable strategy for investors with strong negotiating skills and an understanding of the local real estate market.

How Does Wholesaling Properties Work?

The process of wholesaling properties typically involves the following steps:

Finding distressed property: Investors must find distressed property that is underpriced or in need of repairs. This can involve searching for properties that are in foreclosure, abandoned, or owned by motivated sellers.

Negotiating a contract: Once an investor has found a distressed property, they must negotiate a contract with the seller. This typically involves offering a low price for the property in exchange for a quick sale.

Assigning the contract: After the investor has secured a contract, they can assign the contract to another investor for a fee. This fee is typically a percentage of the purchase price.

Closing the deal: The last step in the process is to close the deal. The buyer will typically pay the purchase price to the seller and the wholesaler will receive their fee.

Benefits of Wholesaling Properties

There are several benefits to wholesaling properties, including:

Minimal risk: Wholesaling properties is a low-risk strategy since investors are not required to own the property or make any repairs.

Quick profits: Wholesaling properties can be a quick way to generate profits since investors can earn a fee for assigning the contract.

No credit or financing required: Investors do not need good credit or financing for wholesale properties, which can make it an attractive strategy for new investors.

Challenges of Wholesaling Properties

While wholesaling properties can be a profitable strategy, there are also some challenges to consider, including:

Finding Good Deals: Finding distressed properties that are underpriced or in need of repairs can be challenging, particularly in a competitive market.

Building a Network: Wholesaling properties requires a network of buyers and sellers, which can take time to build.

Negotiating Skills: Successful wholesalers must have strong negotiating skills to secure contracts at a low price.

Wholesaling properties can be a profitable real estate investing strategy for investors with strong negotiating skills and an understanding of the local real estate market. While there are some challenges to consider, such as finding good deals and building a network, wholesaling properties can be a low-risk way to generate quick profits without requiring good credit or financing. As with any real estate investing strategy, it is important to thoroughly understand the process and risks involved before getting started.

10 - BUYING FORECLOSURE PROPERTIES

Buying foreclosure properties can be a viable strategy for real estate investors looking to purchase properties at a discounted price. Foreclosure properties are homes that have been seized by the bank or other lender after the previous owner was unable to make mortgage payments. These properties are typically sold at auction or through a real estate agent specializing in foreclosures.

However, buying foreclosure properties comes with its own unique set of challenges and risks that investors must be aware of before pursuing this strategy.

One of the main challenges of buying foreclosure properties is competition. Foreclosure properties can be highly desirable to investors looking to purchase properties at a discount, which means that there may be a lot of competition for these properties. This can drive up the price and make it more difficult to find a good deal.

Another challenge of buying foreclosure properties is the condition of the property. Many foreclosure properties have been neglected or damaged by the previous owner, which means that they may require significant repairs and renovations before they can be rented or resold. This can add additional costs and time to the investment process.

In addition to these challenges, there are also legal and financial risks associated with buying foreclosure properties.

Investors must be aware of the legal process involved in purchasing foreclosure property and ensure that they have a

clear understanding of the title and any liens on the

property. They also need to have a clear plan for financing the purchase and any renovations or repairs needed.

Despite these challenges, there are also potential benefits to buying foreclosure properties. The main benefit is the potential for a significant discount on the purchase price. Foreclosure properties are often sold below market value, which means that investors can purchase a property for less than it would normally cost. This can result in a higher return on investment and the potential for long-term capital appreciation.

Another potential benefit of buying foreclosure properties is the ability to negotiate with the lender or bank. Because lenders are often motivated to sell foreclosure properties quickly, investors may be able to negotiate a better deal or more favorable terms.

When considering buying foreclosure properties, it is important for investors to do their due diligence and thoroughly research any potential investments. This includes researching the legal and financial status of the property, assessing its condition, and understanding the local real estate market.

Investors should also have a clear plan for financing the purchase and any renovations or repairs needed. They should also be prepared to actively manage the property, including overseeing tenant relationships, property maintenance, and rental income.

Overall, buying foreclosure properties can be a viable strategy for real estate investors looking to purchase properties at a discount. However, it is important to approach this strategy with a clear understanding of the challenges and risks involved and to do thorough research before making any investment decisions.

Types of Foreclosure Properties

Foreclosure properties can be a profitable investment option for real estate investors. However, not all foreclosures are created equally, and it is important for investors to understand the distinct types of foreclosures and which ones may be the best fit for their investment strategy. In this article, we will discuss the types of foreclosures to purchase when real estate investing.

Pre-Foreclosure Properties

Pre-foreclosure properties are homes that are in the process of foreclosure but have not yet been auctioned off. This means that the homeowner is behind on their mortgage payments and the lender has initiated foreclosure proceedings. However, the property has not yet been foreclosed upon and is still owned by the homeowner.

Investing in pre-foreclosure properties can be a good option for real estate investors who are looking to acquire properties at a discount. Because the homeowner is in financial distress, they may be willing to sell the property for less than its market value. Additionally, because the property has not yet been foreclosed upon, investors may be able to negotiate with the homeowner and work out a deal that benefits both parties.

Auction Properties

Auction properties are homes that have been foreclosed upon and are being sold at a public auction. These properties are typically sold to the highest bidder, and the sale is final.

Investing in auction properties can be a high-risk, high-reward strategy. Because the bidding process is competitive, investors may end up paying more for a property than they had anticipated. However, if the investor can acquire the property at a discount, they may be able to flip it for a profit or hold onto it and rent it out for a steady stream of income.

Bank-Owned Properties

Bank-owned properties, also known as real estate-owned (REO) properties, are homes that have been foreclosed upon and are now owned by the bank. These properties are typically sold through a real estate agent or through an online auction site.

Investing in bank-owned properties can be a good option for investors who are looking for a low-risk investment. Because the bank now owns the property, investors do not need to worry about negotiating with a distressed homeowner.

Additionally, banks are often motivated to sell these properties quickly, which means that investors may be able to acquire them at a discount.

Tax Lien Properties

Tax lien properties are homes that have been seized by the government because the homeowner has failed to pay their property taxes. These properties are sold at auction, and the winning bidder receives a tax lien certificate that gives them the right to collect the unpaid taxes plus interest.

Investing in tax lien properties can be a good option for investors who are looking for a low-risk investment. Because the investor is lending money to the government, there is an insignificant risk of losing their investment. Additionally, if the homeowner eventually pays their back taxes, the investor will receive a return on their investment plus interest.

There are several types of foreclosures to consider when real estate investing, each with its own set of risks and rewards. Investors should carefully consider their investment goals and risk tolerance before deciding which type of foreclosure to pursue. With careful planning and due diligence, investing in foreclosures can be a profitable and rewarding strategy for real estate investors.

Benefits of Buying Foreclosure Properties

Foreclosure properties have long been a popular choice for real estate investors. These properties are often sold at a significant discount, making them an attractive option for those looking to buy low and sell high. However, there are several other benefits to buying foreclosure properties that are worth exploring. In this article, we will discuss some of the most significant benefits of buying foreclosures when real estate investing.

Low Prices

As mentioned, one of the most significant benefits of buying foreclosures is that they are often sold at a significant discount. This is because banks and other lenders are typically more interested in getting rid of the property as quickly as possible than they are in maximizing their profits. This means that buyers can often purchase foreclosure properties for a fraction of their market value, providing a significant opportunity for profit.

Reduced Competition

Because foreclosure properties can be challenging to purchase and require a significant amount of due diligence, many potential buyers may be deterred from pursuing them. This can result in reduced competition for those who are willing to take the time to research and purchase these properties.

Potential for quick turnaround: Because foreclosure properties are often priced well below market value, investors who can purchase them can often sell them quickly for a profit. This can provide a significant opportunity for those looking to make a quick return on their investment.

Opportunity to Improve Properties

Many foreclosure properties have been neglected or poorly maintained, providing an opportunity for investors to purchase them and improve them to increase their value. By renovating or upgrading the property, investors can increase their resale value and maximize their profits.

Potential for Long-term Cash Flow

While many investors focus on flipping foreclosure properties for a quick profit, there is also the potential to hold onto these properties for long-term cash flow. By renting out the property, investors can generate a steady stream of income that can help to offset their initial investment costs.

Access to a Wider Range of Properties

Because foreclosure properties are often sold at a significant discount, investors may be able to access a wider range of properties than they would be able to otherwise. This can provide an opportunity to diversify their portfolio and invest in a range of different properties across different neighborhoods and markets.

Potential for Negotiated Deals

When dealing with foreclosure properties, there may be opportunities to negotiate with the lender or bank that is selling the property. This can result in even further discounts or other favorable terms that can help to increase the investor's potential return on investment.

Overall, buying foreclosure properties can provide a range of benefits for real estate investors. While there are certainly risks and challenges involved, those who are willing to do their due diligence and take the time to research and purchase these properties can potentially reap significant rewards. Whether investors are looking for a quick profit or a long-term cash flow opportunity, buying foreclosure properties can be an excellent way to build wealth through real estate investing.

Challenges of Buying Foreclosure Properties

Buying foreclosed properties can be an attractive opportunity for real estate investors looking for a good deal. Foreclosures can often be purchased at a discount, but they also come with some challenges that investors need to be aware of. In this article, we will explore the challenges of buying foreclosures and what investors should be aware of before diving in.

Competition

Foreclosed properties are highly sought after by investors and homebuyers alike, which means there is often a lot of competition. Investors may find themselves in bidding wars with other buyers, which can drive up the price and decrease the potential profit. It is important for investors to have a solid understanding of the market and to be prepared to act quickly to secure a good deal.

Condition

Foreclosed properties are often sold as-is, which means that investors may be purchasing a property with significant repairs needed. Investors need to be aware of the potential costs associated with fixing up a foreclosed property and factor those costs into their investment calculations. It is also important to have a thorough inspection of the property before making an offer to identify any potential issues.

Liens and Back Taxes

Foreclosed properties may come with liens or back taxes

owed, which can complicate the sale process. Investors need to conduct thorough due diligence to identify any potential liens or back taxes and factor those costs into their investment calculations. If liens or back taxes are discovered after the sale, the new owner may be responsible for paying them off.

Delays

Buying a foreclosed property can be a lengthy process, which can create delays in the investment timeline. There may be delays in obtaining financing, obtaining clear title, or in closing the sale. Investors need to be prepared for potential delays and have a solid understanding of the timeline involved in purchasing a foreclosed property.

Occupancy

Foreclosed properties may be occupied by the previous owner or tenants, which can create additional challenges. If the property is occupied, the new owner may be required to go through the eviction process to gain possession of the property. This can be a time-consuming and costly process that can delay the investment timeline.

Title Issues

Foreclosed properties may have title issues that need to be addressed before the sale can be completed. This can include issues such as boundary disputes, easements, or other encumbrances in the title. Investors need to conduct thorough due diligence to identify any potential title issues and work with a qualified attorney to address them.

Financing

Financing a foreclosed property can be challenging, particularly if the property is in poor condition. Traditional lenders may be hesitant to provide financing for a property that needs significant repairs, which can limit the pool of potential buyers. Investors may need to explore alternative financing options, such as hard money loans, to secure financing for a foreclosed property.

Market Conditions

The real estate market is constantly changing, which means that the value of a foreclosed property may fluctuate over time. Investors need to have a solid understanding of the local real estate market and be prepared to adjust their investment strategy based on changing market conditions.

Lack of Information

Foreclosed properties may not have complete or accurate information available, which can make it difficult for investors to make informed decisions. Investors need to conduct thorough due diligence and work with qualified professionals to identify potential issues and assess the potential value of the property. Emotional Investment

Investors may become emotionally invested in a foreclosed property, which can cloud their judgment and lead to poor investment decisions. It is important for investors to remain objective and make investment decisions based on the numbers, not on emotions.

11 - BECOMING A PRIVATE MONEY LENDER

Private money lending can be a profitable business for individuals who have access to capital and are willing to invest in real estate. In 2023, private money lending can offer investors an opportunity to earn a return on their investment while helping others fund their real estate projects. Here is what you need to know about becoming a private money lender:

What is Private Money Lending?

Private money lending is a form of financing in which an individual or company lends money to real estate investors or developers. The loans are secured by the property being purchased or renovated, and the terms of the loan are negotiated between the lender and borrower.

As a private money lender, you can earn a return on your investment by charging interest on the loan. The interest rate and terms of the loan will depend on the borrower's creditworthiness, the type of property being purchased or renovated, and the market conditions.

How to Become a Private Money Lender

If you are interested in becoming a private money lender, here are the steps you can take:

Evaluate your financial situation: Private money lending

requires access to capital. Evaluate your financial situation to determine how much you can invest and how much risk you are willing to take on.

Research the market: Research the real estate market to determine the types of properties that are in demand and the areas that are experiencing growth.

Find potential borrowers: Network with real estate investors and developers to find potential borrowers who are looking for financing.

Evaluate Potential Borrowers

Before lending money to a borrower, evaluate their creditworthiness, experience in real estate investing, and the viability of their project.

Negotiate Loan Terms

Once you have found a potential borrower, negotiate the terms of the loan, including the interest rate, fees, and repayment schedule.

Fund the Loan

If you agree to the terms, fund the loan,and secure the loan with the property being purchased or renovated.

Becoming a Certified Private Money

Lender with Lee Arnold

This is how I learned more about being a Private Money Lender. Just keep in mind that you do not have to be certified to be a money lender and this class is not free.

Aspiring private money lenders who want to enter the real estate lending industry can become certified by undergoing training and mentorship programs. One such program is offered by Lee Arnold, a successful private money lender, and real estate investment expert.

Lee Arnold's program is designed to provide aspiring private money lenders with a comprehensive education on the lending industry, as well as the skills and knowledge they need to be successful lenders. The program includes several modules covering topics such as the fundamentals of real estate lending, underwriting,and evaluating potential deals, mitigating risk, and managing a lending portfolio.

To Become a Certified Private Money

Lender Research the Program

The first step in becoming a certified private money lender with Lee Arnold is to research the program and familiarize yourself with the curriculum, requirements, and costs. Lee Arnold's program is available online, and participants can learn at their own pace, making it ideal for individuals who have full-time jobs or other commitments.

Complete the Coursework

After enrolling in the program, participants must complete the coursework, which typically consists of online video lectures, readings, and assignments. The coursework covers topics such as the lending process, risk mitigation, due diligence, and deal structuring.

Attend the Mentorship Program: In addition to the coursework, participants must also attend a mentorship program, which is typically held over several days. During the mentorship program, participants will have the opportunity to meet with Lee Arnold and other successful private money lenders, as well as learn more about the lending industry and best practices for success.

Pass the Certification Exam

After completing the coursework and mentorship program, participants must pass a certification exam to become a certified private money lender. The exam typically covers the material covered in the coursework and mentorship program, and tests participants' knowledge of the lending industry and best practices.

Start Lending

Once certified, private money lenders can begin lending to real estate investors and borrowers. Lee Arnold's program provides ongoing support to certified lenders, including access to deal flow, due diligence support, and other resources to help them succeed in the industry.

Becoming a certified private money lender with Lee Arnold can be a terrific way to enter the real estate lending industry and build a successful lending portfolio. However, it is important to note that the process requires a significant investment of time and money, as well as a willingness to learn and adapt to the constantly changing lending landscape.

Additional Tips

Build a Network

Building a network of real estate investors, brokers, and other industry professionals can be crucial to success as a private money lender. Networking can help you find potential borrowers and investors, as well as provide valuable insights into the market and lending opportunities.

Focus on Due Diligence

One of the most important aspects of successful real estate lending is conducting thorough due diligence on potential deals. This includes evaluating the borrower's financial situation, assessing the property's value, and analyzing the market and economic conditions.

Stay Informed

The real estate lending industry is constantly evolving, and it is important to stay informed about current trends, regulations, and best practices. Reading industry publications, attending conferences and events, and staying up to date on market conditions can help you stay ahead of the curve and make informed lending decisions.

Manage Risk

As with any investment, there is always risk involved in real estate lending. Successful private money lenders manage risk by diversifying their portfolio, conducting thorough due diligence, and carefully analyzing each potential deal.

Once you have a solid understanding of the lending process, it is time to evaluate deals and make offers. To do this effectively, you will need to understand the basics of real estate analysis and property valuation. This will involve learning how to read financial statements, analyze market data, and evaluate property conditions.

Lee Arnold offers comprehensive training on how to evaluate deals and make offers, including guidance on creating a property analysis report, using deal analysis software, and negotiating with borrowers.

Closing Deals and Servicing Loans

Once you have identified a promising deal and evaluated its potential, it is time to close the loan and begin servicing it. This involves conducting due diligence, coordinating with title companies and attorneys, and ensuring that all legal requirements are met.

Lee Arnold provides training on the closing process, including how to prepare loan documents, conduct due diligence, and coordinate with title companies and attorneys.

He also offers guidance on how to service loans, including how to collect payments, manage escrow accounts, and handle default situations.

Scaling Your Private Lending Business

Once you have established a successful private lending business, you may want to consider scaling it up. This can involve expanding your lending portfolio, developing innovative marketing strategies, and building a team of professionals to help you manage your business.

Lee Arnold provides guidance on how to scale your private lending business, including how to develop a marketing plan, manage your lending portfolio, and recruit and train team members.

Continuing Education and Networking

To stay on top of industry trends and best practices, it is important to engage in ongoing education and networking. This can involve attending industry conferences, reading industry publications, and connecting with other private lenders.

Lee Arnold offers opportunities for ongoing education and networking through his training programs, as well as through his company, The Lee Arnold System of Real Estate Investing.

The company hosts regular events and conferences and provides access to a network of private lenders and real estate investors.

Benefits of Private Money Lending

Private money lending has become a popular alternative to traditional financing in recent years, with many investors seeing the benefits of becoming a private money lender.

Here are some of the key reasons why:

Higher Returns: Private money lenders typically receive higher returns on their investments than traditional lenders. This is because private money lenders are taking on more risk by lending to borrowers who may not qualify for traditional financing. In return for this risk, private money lenders can charge higher interest rates and fees. These higher returns can be extremely attractive to investors looking for passive income streams.

Diversification: Investing in real estate through private money lending provides investors with a way to diversify their portfolio. By spreading their investment across multiple loans, investors can minimize their risk and increase their chances of generating consistent returns. Diversification can also help investors weather economic downturns or market fluctuations.

Control: As a private money lender, you have more control over your investments than if you were investing in stocks or mutual funds. You can choose which loans to invest in, set your own terms, and have a direct say in how your money is being used. This level of control can give investors greater peace of mind and a sense of ownership over their investments.

Passive Income: Private money lending provides investors with a way to earn passive income. Unlike traditional real estate investing, which requires active management, private money lending allows investors to earn a return on their investment without having to manage properties or deal with tenants. This makes it an attractive option for investors who want to generate income without being tied down to a particular location or property.

Flexibility: Private money lending is a flexible investment strategy that can be tailored to meet the individual needs of investors. You can choose to invest in a single loan or spread your investment across multiple loans. You can also choose the terms of your investment, such as the interest rate, the duration of the loan, and the type of property being financed.

Security: Private money lending is typically secured by the property being financed, which provides investors with an added layer of security. If the borrower defaults on the loan, the lender can take possession of the property and sell it to recoup their investment. This means that private money lending can be a low-risk investment strategy, especially if the lender has a good understanding of the local real estate market and the properties being financed.

Access to Deals: As a private money lender, you have access to a wide range of real estate deals that may not be available to traditional investors. This is because private money lending allows borrowers to finance properties that may not meet the strict lending criteria of traditional banks. This can include properties that need significant repairs or renovations, or properties that have a higher risk of default.

Overall, private money lending can be a highly beneficial investment strategy for those looking to earn higher returns, diversify their portfolio, and have greater control over their investments. However, it is important to understand the risks involved and to have a good understanding of the local real estate market before investing. Working with an experienced private money lending company or mentor like Lee Arnold can also be helpful in navigating the complex world of private money lending.

12 - THE LUCRATIVE NATURE OF REAL

ESTATE INVESTING

In 2023, the real estate market continues to offer investors many opportunities for growth and profitability. Real estate investing is a lucrative business that has made many investors wealthy. The profits that can be generated in real estate investing are higher than many other forms of investment, including stocks, bonds, and mutual funds. However, the level of success that a real estate investor achieves depends on their knowledge, experience, and the strategies they employ.

One of the main benefits of real estate investing is that it provides investors with the opportunity to generate cash flow through rental income. When a real estate investor purchases a property, they can rent it out to tenants, which provides them with a consistent stream of income. The amount of rental income that a property generates depends on the location and demand for rental properties in the area.

In addition to generating cash flow through rental income, real estate investors can also make profits through appreciation. Appreciation refers to the increase in the value of a property over time. Real estate values tend to appreciate over the long-term, which means that investors can make significant profits when they sell a property that has appreciated in value.

Another benefit of real estate investing is that it provides investors with tax advantages. Real estate investors can take advantage of tax deductions, including depreciation, mortgage interest, property taxes, and maintenance expenses. These deductions can help to reduce the investor's tax liability, which can increase their overall profitability.

Real estate investing also provides investors with the opportunity to leverage their investments. When a real estate investor purchases a property with a mortgage, they can use the rental income from the property to pay off the mortgage. This means that the investor can purchase more properties with the same amount of initial investment, which can increase their overall profits. One of the reasons why real estate investing is so lucrative is that it is a tangible asset. Unlike stocks and bonds, which are intangible assets, real estate is a physical asset that can be seen and touched. This makes it more valuable to many investors, as they can physically see and understand the value of their investment.

Real estate investing can also provide investors with the opportunity to diversify their portfolio. By investing in several types of real estate, such as commercial properties, residential properties, and land, investors can spread their risk and increase their chances of making profits.

Despite the many benefits of real estate investing, it is important to note that it is not without its risks. Real estate markets can be volatile, and property values can fluctuate overtime. In addition, real estate investments require a significant amount of capital, which can be a barrier to entry for some investors.

Moreover, real estate investors need to be aware of the risks associated with managing properties. Tenants can cause damage to properties, and landlords can face legal issues if they do not comply with local laws and regulations. Real estate investors also need to be aware of the risks associated with financing properties, including the risk of defaulting on a mortgage.

To be successful in real estate investing, investors need to have a solid understanding of the market and the strategies that are most effective in generating profits. They also need to be aware of the risks associated with investing in real estate and take steps to mitigate those risks.

Real estate investing is a lucrative business that can provide investors with a range of benefits, including cash flow, appreciation, tax advantages, and the opportunity to leverage their investments. However, it is important to be aware of the risks associated with real estate investing and to take steps to mitigate those risks. With the right knowledge and experience, real estate investors can generate significant profits and build wealth over the long-term.

13 - INVESTING ANYWHERE

Real estate investing is not limited to your local market. With the advancements in technology and communication, it is now possible to invest in real estate from anywhere in the world. Here are some ways to invest in real estate from any location:

Online Real Estate Marketplaces

Online real estate marketplaces, such as Roofstock and Fundrise, allow investors to purchase shares in pre-vetted rental properties. These platforms offer the convenience of investing in real estate without the hassle of property management. Additionally, online real estate marketplaces provide investors with access to investment opportunities across the country, allowing them to diversify their portfolio.

Real Estate Investment Trusts (REITs)

One of the easiest ways to invest in real estate is through Real Estate Investment Trusts (REITs). REITs are companies that own or finance income-generating real estate, such as apartment buildings, office spaces, and shopping centers.

REITs allow investors to invest in real estate without owning the property themselves. Instead, investors can purchase shares in a REIT, which pays dividends based on the rental income generated by the properties it owns. REITs are an attractive option for those who want to invest in real estate but do not have the time, resources, or knowledge to manage a property themselves.

Syndications and Crowdfunding

Real estate crowdfunding has become increasingly popular in recent years. This involves pooling funds from multiple investors to invest in a specific real estate project. The investment is typically facilitated through an online platform, and investors can contribute as little as a few hundred dollars. Real estate crowdfunding provides access to investment opportunities that may have previously been out of reach for individual investors. However, it is important to note that investing in real estate crowdfunding comes with risks, including the potential for project delays or failure.

Syndications and crowdfunding platforms, such as CrowdStreet and RealtyMogul, allow investors to pool their resources and invest in larger real estate projects. These platforms provide access to institutional-grade investments that were previously only available to wealthy investors.

Property Management Companies

Property management companies can be a great option for those who want to invest in real estate but do not have the time or resources to manage a property themselves. These companies offer a variety of services, including finding tenants, collecting rent, and handling maintenance and repairs. By working with a property management company, investors can generate rental income without the responsibilities of being a landlord.

Real Estate Investment Clubs

Real estate investment clubs provide a forum for investors to network, share knowledge, and pool resources to invest in real estate. These clubs often hold meetings, seminars, and events to educate members on real estate investing and provide access to investment opportunities. By joining an investment club, investors can learn from experienced investors and gain access to investment opportunities they may not have found on their own.

Hire a Local Property Manager

If you want to invest in rental properties in a specific location, but do not live there, you can hire a local property manager to manage the property on your behalf. A property manager can handle tasks such as tenant screening, rent collection, and maintenance, allowing you to invest in properties remotely.

Real estate investing is no longer limited to your local market. With the advancements in technology and communication, investors can now invest in real estate from anywhere in the world. Online real estate marketplaces, REITs, syndications, crowdfunding, and hiring a local property manager are all strategies that investors can use to invest in real estate from any location. Regardless of the strategy you choose, it is important to conduct thorough due diligence and work with professionals who can help you assess the risks and potential returns of each investment opportunity.

It can be challenging to manage properties in an area where you do not reside. That is why it is essential to find and hire a reliable property manager who can handle the day-to-day operations of your rental properties. In this article, we will discuss how to find and hire a property manager when investing in an area that you do not reside in.

Research Property Management Companies

The first step in finding a property manager is to research property management companies in the area where your rental properties are located. You can start by searching online or asking for referrals from other real estate investors in the area. Once you have compiled a list of potential property management companies, you should review their websites, read customer reviews, and check their credentials.

Check Their Licenses and Certifications

It is crucial to ensure that the property management company you hire is licensed and certified. In many states, property managers are required to hold a real estate broker's license or a property management license. You can check with your state's real estate regulatory agency to confirm the property management company's license and credentials.

Interview Potential Property Managers

After narrowing down your list of potential property management companies, you should schedule interviews with them. During the interview, you should make sure to ask questions about their experience managing rental properties, their communication and reporting processes, their tenant screening process, and their fees. You should also ask for references and check them.

Review the Management Agreement

Once you have selected a property management company, they will provide you with a management agreement. Review the agreement carefully to ensure that it includes all the services you need, the fees and payment schedule, the length of the agreement, and the process for terminating the agreement. If you have any questions or concerns, you should discuss them with the property management company before signing the agreement.

Establish Communication Processes

Effective communication is crucial in any business relationship, and it is no different when it comes to working with a property management company. You should establish communication processes with your property manager, including how frequently they will update you on the status of your properties, how they will handle maintenance requests and emergencies, and how they will handle rental payments.

Monitor the Property Manager's Performance

After you have hired a property manager, it is essential to monitor their performance regularly. You should review their reports and financial statements, evaluate tenant satisfaction, and monitor the condition of your properties. If you notice any issues or concerns, you should address them to the property manager promptly.

In summary, finding and hiring a reliable property manager is crucial when investing in an area where you do not reside. By researching property management companies, checking their licenses and certifications, interviewing potential property managers, reviewing the management agreement, establishing communication processes, and monitoring the property manager's performance, you can ensure that your rental properties are well-managed and profitable.

14 - BE A GREAT LANDLORD

Being a great landlord is not an easy task, and it requires more than just collecting rent. A great landlord should be not only knowledgeable but also personable, reliable, and approachable. Here are some tips on how to be a great landlord:

Know the Laws in your State

As a landlord, it is essential to know the local and state laws that govern landlord-tenant relationships. You should be familiar with tenant rights, eviction processes, and property maintenance regulations.

Screen Tenants Thoroughly

Before renting out your property, you need to screen your potential tenants thoroughly. This includes running background checks, checking credit scores, verifying income, and speaking to references. This helps you to ensure that you are renting to reliable and responsible tenants.

Keep the Property Well-Maintained

A well-maintained property not only attracts good tenants but also helps to maintain the value of your investment.

Regular maintenance such as cleaning, painting, and repairs should be done promptly.

Be Responsive

As a landlord, you should be responsive to your tenants' needs and concerns. Promptly addressing maintenance issues and being available for questions or concerns helps to establish a good landlord-tenant relationship.

Respect Tenants' Privacy

Tenants have a right to privacy, and you should respect that right. Give tenants reasonable notice before entering the property, except in the case of emergencies.

Communicate Clearly

Clear communication between you and your tenants is crucial. Make sure to provide clear instructions on how to pay rent, report maintenance issues, and any other essential information.

Provide Amenities

Providing amenities such as laundry facilities, storage, and parking can help make your property more attractive to potential tenants.

Handle Complaints Professionally

When a tenant has a complaint, it's important to handle it professionally and objectively. Take the time to listen to their concerns and work to find a mutually satisfactory resolution.

Be Flexible

Being flexible with lease terms, move-in dates, and other aspects of the rental process can help to attract good tenants and establish a positive relationship.

Show Appreciation

Showing appreciation to your tenants for being responsible and reliable can help to strengthen the landlord-tenant relationship. Simple gestures such as sending a thank-you note or providing a small gift can go a long way.